THE
BIG SHIFT
STUDY JOURNAL

Copyright © 2024 by Dr. J Calaway

Published by Four Rivers Media

All rights reserved. No portion of this book may be reproduced, stored in a retrieval system, or transmitted in any form or by any means—electronic, mechanical, photocopy, recording, scanning, or other—except for brief quotations in critical reviews or articles, without prior written permission of the author.

Scripture quotations marked AMP are taken from the Amplified® Bible (AMP), Copyright © 2015 by The Lockman Foundation. Used by permission. www.lockman.org | Scripture quotations marked MSG are taken from THE MESSAGE, copyright © 1993, 1994, 1995, 1996, 2000, 2001, 2002 by Eugene H. Peterson. Used by permission of NavPress. All rights reserved. Represented by Tyndale House Publishers, Inc. | Scripture quotations marked NIV are taken from the Holy Bible, New International Version®, NIV®. Copyright © 1973, 1978, 1984, 2011 by Biblica, Inc.™ Used by permission of Zondervan. All rights reserved worldwide. www.zondervan.com. The "NIV" and "New International Version" are trademarks registered in the United States Patent and Trademark Office by Biblica, Inc.™ | Scripture quotations marked NLT are taken from the Holy Bible, New Living Translation, copyright © 1996, 2004, 2015 by Tyndale House Foundation. Used by permission of Tyndale House Publishers, Inc., Carol Stream, Illinois 60188. All rights reserved. | Scripture quotations marked TPT are from The Passion Translation®. Copyright © 2017, 2018 by Passion & Fire Ministries, Inc. Used by permission. All rights reserved. ThePassionTranslation.com |

For foreign and subsidiary rights, contact the author.

Cover design by Sara Young
Cover photo by Melanie Latiak

ISBN: 978-1-962401-91-3   1 2 3 4 5 6 7 8 9 10

Printed in the United States of America

STUDY JOURNAL

THE
BIG SHIFT

DR. J CALAWAY

CONTENTS

CHAPTER 1. Introduction 6

CHAPTER 2. Exit 2's and Orange Roofed Hotels 10

CHAPTER 3. Revolving Doors and Mustang Cobras 14

CHAPTER 4. That's What I Saw 22

CHAPTER 5. Setting Bone, Mending Nets, and Healing Factions 28

CHAPTER 6. The Strategy of a Diligent Leader 34

CHAPTER 7. Last Man Standing and Lonely Roads 42

CHAPTER 8. The Divine New: Mavericks and Managers ... 48

CHAPTER 9. Fish, Gold Coins, and Doctors 54

INTRODUCTION

> Change isn't just knocking on our door; it's doing a full-on dance routine on our welcome mat.

READING TIME

As you read the introduction of *The Big Shift*, review, reflect on, and respond to the text by answering the following questions.

REFLECT AND TAKE ACTION:

How do you reconcile comfort and the inevitability of change? How open are you to the certainty of change?

_____
_____
_____
_____
_____
_____
_____
_____
_____

How clear is your vision, and what role has it played in moving you forward amid disruption and pandemonium?

_____
_____
_____
_____
_____
_____
_____
_____
_____

How well has the structure of your organization adapted to times of transition and rapid change? What reasons do you attribute to times when your structure has collapsed versus times when your structure withstood the pressures of change?

_____
_____
_____
_____
_____
_____
_____
_____
_____
_____

The author declares that "sacrifice isn't martyrdom; it's an investment." What kind of sacrificial investments have you made for the sake of healthy transformation, and in what ways have they paid off?

_____
_____
_____
_____
_____
_____
_____
_____
_____
_____

The author mentions the necessity of "Issachar Insight" as described in 1 Chronicles 12:32 in today's ever-changing world. What do you foresee coming around the bend in the future, and how will it impact the way you lead? What implications does that have on your organization?

_____
_____
_____
_____
_____
_____
_____
_____
_____
_____
_____
_____

CHAPTER 1

EXIT 2'S AND ORANGE ROOFED HOTELS

> The days of resting on our historic laurels and glorying in the past are over.

READING TIME

As you read Chapter 1: "Exit 2's and Orange Roofed Hotels" in *The Big Shift*, review, reflect on, and respond to the text by answering the following questions.

REVIEW, REFLECT, AND RESPOND

The author describes the coexistence of comfort and restlessness that he and his wife experienced before their lives changed. In what ways do you relate to this? How have you responded to this coexistence in the past, and what was the end result?

_____
_____
_____
_____
_____
_____
_____
_____

Refer to the author's story of the vision God gave him through the leadership of a senior pastor. Who is God using in your life right now to point you in a specific direction? Describe what you think God is trying to accomplish in you as a leader.

_____
_____
_____
_____
_____
_____
_____
_____

Read the first leadership lesson #1. In your own words, explain why the lead or senior minister is central to the vision, leadership, and advancement of the church. What have you observed in churches or organizations where this principle is not upheld?

_____
_____
_____
_____
_____
_____
_____
_____

The second leadership lesson #1 says that God doesn't call us to churches. What does that mean? How does the author's story about the car wreck and hotel support this principle?

_____
_____
_____
_____
_____
_____
_____
_____
_____

The author cautions leaders to be ready to shift at any time in the third leadership lesson #1. What do you think that posture of readiness looks like practically?

_____
_____
_____
_____
_____
_____
_____
_____

This chapter quotes John F. Kennedy as saying, "Things do not simply happen. They are made to happen." What role does God play in that? What role do you play?

_____
_____
_____
_____
_____
_____
_____
_____

CHAPTER 2

REVOLVING DOORS AND MUSTANG COBRAS

> Once you know what's stopping you, you can figure out how to move it out of the way.

READING TIME

As you read Chapter 2: "Revolving Doors and Mustang Cobras" in The Big Shift, review, reflect on, and respond to the text by answering the following questions.

REVIEW, REFLECT, AND RESPOND

As a leader, how did you make sense of the dramatic shifts in the church from COVID-19, and how did it impact the way you do ministry? Describe what you learned along the way, noting how your perspectives and methods evolved.

_____
_____
_____
_____
_____
_____
_____
_____

How did you respond to the conflicting voices on how to handle church during COVID-19? Are you satisfied with the way you responded? Why or why not? What would you have done differently?

_____
_____
_____
_____
_____
_____
_____

> **"Be alert, be present. I'm about to do something new. It's bursting out! Don't you see it?"**
>
> —Isaiah 43:19 (MSG)

Consider the scripture above and answer the following questions:

Reflect on a time when you may have missed the work God was doing in your ministry because of poor awareness or distraction. How did this impact your leadership in your church or organization?

_____
_____
_____
_____
_____
_____
_____

What does God's command to "be alert" and "be present" bring to mind as it pertains to your organization? What is the new thing God wants to do? Are you allowing it? Why or why not?

_____
_____
_____
_____
_____
_____
_____
_____

This scripture suggests that God makes it obvious when He intends to do something new, yet we often miss it. Why do you think that discrepancy exists?

_____
_____
_____
_____
_____
_____
_____
_____
_____
_____
_____

The decisions the author made during COVID-19 launched GateHubs. Consider the greatest shift or change your church or organization is facing right now. What kind of great things do you think God will do with the brokenness and rubble? Where do you see potential?

_____
_____
_____
_____
_____
_____
_____
_____
_____
_____
_____

The first leadership lesson #1 in this chapter is "Pay attention." What is God stirring in you and around you to awaken you to the new things He wants to do?

_____
_____
_____
_____
_____
_____
_____
_____
_____

How would you describe the difference between a shift and a pivot? Provide a personal example of each.

_____
_____
_____
_____
_____
_____
_____
_____
_____

The second leadership lesson #1 is "Just because you challenge something doesn't mean you're against it. There might simply be a better way." Can you identify something in your organization that has been working but could work better? What would it look like to refine it?

_____
_____
_____
_____
_____
_____
_____
_____

The third leadership lesson #1 is "Be willing to disengage to reengage." Why do you think true engagement first requires disengagement?

_____
_____
_____
_____
_____
_____
_____
_____

The fourth leadership lesson #1 is "When you sense the new shift of God, don't try to figure it out. Just pray—A LOT!" Think of a time when you entered into "figure it out" mode during a big shift. Did it accomplish what you were hoping to accomplish?

_____
_____
_____
_____
_____
_____
_____
_____

How do you strike a balance between letting God "figure it out" and maintaining your own sense of purpose and direction to avoid drifting?

_____
_____
_____
_____
_____
_____
_____
_____

How does your church or ministry demonstrate itself as the *kubernasis* of the community in conscience, conviction, compassion, community, and corporate functioning? Where do you see a need for improvement?

___

Consider the final leadership lesson #1 in this chapter: "Good leaders know what battles to fight. Great leaders know when to fight them." What important battles have you had to fight in the past, and what role did timing play in them?

___

CHAPTER 3

THAT'S WHAT I SAW

Always begin with the end in mind.

READING TIME

As you read Chapter 3: "That's What I Saw" in *The Big Shift*, review, reflect on, and respond to the text by answering the following questions.

REVIEW, REFLECT, AND RESPOND

The first leadership lesson #1 of this chapter is "To make a shift a reality, you must see it before you can live it." What do you envision as the end result of a shift you'd like to make in your ministry and/or organization? Describe what you see.

_____
_____
_____
_____
_____
_____
_____

What does it mean to become irrelevant in the context of the modern landscape of the church today?

_____
_____
_____
_____
_____
_____
_____

> *"A man's mind plans his way [as he journeys through life], but the LORD directs his steps and establishes him."*
>
> —Proverbs 16:9 (AMP)

Consider the scripture above and answer the following questions:

In accordance with the second leadership lesson #1, this scripture denotes the inherent collaboration between man and God in creating new things. In what ways are you collaborating with the Lord to establish what's next for your church or organization?

_____
_____
_____
_____
_____
_____

What is the last thing the Lord has asked you to do? In what direction do you sense His leading? How closely do the plans of your heart seem to line up with the direction God is taking you?

_____
_____
_____
_____
_____
_____
_____

The third leadership lesson #1 warns leaders not to worship methods or confuse them with vision. How does the author's distinction between vision and methods inform the way you think about change?

_____
_____
_____
_____
_____
_____
_____
_____
_____
_____

Using the author's statements and elements as a model, devise a vision and mission statement for your organization.

_____
_____
_____
_____
_____
_____
_____
_____
_____
_____

What core values guide your church day-to-day? How well are these values being carried out by the leaders in your organization?

___

What makes your vision challenging yet attainable?

___

Ask your team to tell you what they think the organization's vision is. What did they say? Are there any discrepancies between your understanding of the vision and theirs?

___

_____
_____
_____
_____

What are your team members learning as you work together to sustain the vision in and through organizational shifts?

_____
_____
_____
_____
_____
_____

The fourth leadership lesson #1 advises to "be open and flexible with whom you enlist on the team." What does your organization need that you don't currently have? Who on your team may be coachable and able to meet that need?

_____
_____
_____
_____
_____
_____

CHAPTER 4

SETTING BONE, MENDING NETS, AND HEALING FACTIONS

> That's okay, the public perception that Jesus was dead and not coming back was real as well.

READING TIME

As you read Chapter 4: "Setting Bone, Mending Nets, and Healing Factions" in *The Big Shift*, review, reflect on, and respond to the text by answering the following questions.

REVIEW, REFLECT, AND RESPOND

Prior to reading this chapter, what did organizational "structure" and "governance" mean to you? How would you describe the structure and governance within your own organization? How robust are they?

_____
_____
_____
_____
_____
_____
_____

On a scale from 1 to 10 (1 = not at all fluid, 10 = extremely fluid), where does the governance and structure of your church or organization fall? Why did you score them the way you did?

1   2   3   4   5   6   7   8   9   10

_____
_____
_____
_____
_____
_____

Consider the five gifts/offices that God calls to equip the church (apostle, prophet, evangelist, pastor, and teacher). How well does your church mirror this design?

_____
_____
_____
_____
_____
_____
_____

> *"I became weak to win the weak. I have adapted to the culture of every place I've gone so that I could more easily win people to Christ."*
>
> —1 Corinthians 9:22 (TPT)

Consider the scripture above and answer the following questions:

In what ways does this scripture speak to the inevitability of sacrifice in the process of working with the limitations of tradition to welcome the new?

_____
_____
_____
_____
_____
_____
_____
_____
_____

How could you apply Paul's message to your efforts to balance tradition and innovation? How might this approach impact your team's receptivity to innovation?

_____
_____
_____
_____
_____
_____
_____

Who determines the structure and establishes clear lines of authority in your organization?

_____
_____
_____
_____
_____

Read through the six factors that make organizational structure and governance important during a shift (clarity and focus, decision-making and agility, resource allocation and optimization, communication and collaboration, risk management and compliance, and learning and adaptability). In which of these do your greatest strengths and weaknesses fall?

_____
_____
_____
_____
_____
_____

Refer to the three corporate governance models (community, core and committed, and stewardship). What stands out to you about these models? Which model do you tend to focus on the most? What would it look like to develop a more well-rounded governance model?

_____
_____
_____
_____
_____
_____
_____

In what ways does your organization adhere to a leader-focused and follower-focused structure? Which of the listed advantages and disadvantages of each have emerged in your organization or church? Answer the key questions the author lists to assist you in striking a balance between the two.

_____
_____
_____
_____
_____
_____
_____

What are the core traditions of your church/organization? How are you building new ideas on top of those strong traditional foundations?

_____
_____

Take some time to answer the final six questions listed at the conclusion of this chapter to determine where balance is needed in your organization. How do your answers help you to make sense of the imbalances in your organization, and what steps can you take to find balance?

What did you learn about structure and governance that you didn't know or understand before? How will you apply it to your organization moving forward?

CHAPTER 5

THE STRATEGY OF A DILIGENT LEADER

> The leader who is content with "what is" and not focused on "what could be" isn't a leader but a manager of today.

READING TIME

As you read Chapter 5: "The Strategy of a Diligent Leader" in *The Big Shift*, review, reflect on, and respond to the text by answering the following questions.

REVIEW, REFLECT, AND RESPOND

What comes to mind when you think of the Diligent Leader? What Diligent Leaders do you know, and what about them makes them Diligent Leaders?

_____
_____
_____
_____
_____
_____
_____
_____

What do you think makes you a leader? Did you pursue leadership, or were you thrust into it? How has your entrance into leadership shaped you into the leader you are today?

_____
_____
_____
_____
_____
_____
_____
_____

> *"But I say walk habitually in the [Holy] Spirit [seek Him and be responsive to His guidance], and then you will certainly not carry out the desire of the sinful nature [which responds impulsively without regard for God and His precepts]."*
>
> —Galatians 5:16 (AMP)

Consider the scripture above and answer the following questions:

In what way does this scripture personify the Diligent Leader?

_____
_____
_____
_____
_____
_____
_____

In the context of the entire chapter, in what ways might impulsivity and negligence of Holy Spirit's leading prevent a leader from displaying the characteristics of a Diligent Leader?

_____
_____
_____
_____
_____
_____
_____
_____

Answer the following questions based on the ten traits of Diligent Leadership (launch, establish, assist, deliver, equalize, resilient, stand, honor, integrity, protection):

What haven't you launched that needs to be launched? Based on the first step (communicating the launch), how could you execute it? To what extent have you communicated with the five groups of influencers if you have already initiated the launch?

_____
_____
_____
_____
_____
_____
_____
_____
_____
_____

What tends to hold you back from acting on your vision?

_____
_____
_____
_____
_____
_____
_____
_____
_____
_____

Review the A's of assisting your team through a big shift. Describe in detail the ways in which you pay attention, affirm them, and help them apply what they learn. Where could you make improvements?

_____
_____
_____
_____
_____
_____
_____

How do you think your people would rate you on your follow-through of your promises?

_____
_____
_____
_____
_____
_____

In what ways does your dedication come through as you work to complete your mission?

_____
_____
_____
_____

_____
_____
_____

How decisive are you in making difficult decisions? Consider a decision that you need to make right now. What's the worst thing that could happen if you made the wrong decision?

_____
_____
_____
_____
_____
_____
_____

In what areas of your life do you lack discipline? How might greater discipline in that area impact the way you lead during a shift?

_____
_____
_____
_____
_____
_____
_____

In what ways do you embody both the pathfinder and the pioneer?

_____
_____
_____
_____
_____
_____

What does resiliency look like in your leadership? Provide an example and explain how it helped you accomplish your vision.

_____
_____
_____
_____
_____
_____

How does losing momentum impact your endurance to finish what you started? How does the author's charge to stand comfort or encourage you?

_____
_____
_____
_____

_____
_____
_____
_____
_____

How do you hold your team and organization together as you lead through seasons of change?

_____
_____
_____
_____
_____
_____
_____
_____

In what ways are you protecting other leaders, your followers, and the organization's brand?

_____
_____
_____
_____
_____
_____
_____

CHAPTER 6

LAST MAN STANDING AND LONELY ROADS

> The more I focus on the loss or sacrifice, the less I see the gains and blessings.

READING TIME

As you read Chapter 6: "Last Man Standing and Lonely Roads" in *The Big Shift*, review, reflect on, and respond to the text by answering the following questions.

REVIEW, REFLECT, AND RESPOND

How do you respond to loss or the threat of loss as a leader? How does it impact your openness and willingness to make necessary shifts in your life and your organization?

_____
_____
_____
_____
_____
_____
_____
_____

In your own words, how would you describe the difference between balance and rhythm? Do your work and personal life more closely reflect efforts toward balance or rhythm?

_____
_____
_____
_____
_____
_____
_____
_____

> *"Not my will, but Yours be done."*
> —Luke 22:42 (NIV)

Consider the scripture above and answer the following questions:

Think of a time when you made leadership decisions that changed the course of the organization, for better or for worse. Whose will was being done?

_____
_____
_____
_____

How do you know when you are following God's will versus your own as you navigate big organizational changes?

_____
_____
_____
_____

According to the first leadership lesson #1 in this chapter, "Life at times will be out of balance, and that's okay." How do you respond to seasons of imbalance? How could you break that cycle?

_____
_____
_____
_____

The second leadership lesson #1 advises focusing on being in rhythm when things are out of balance. Think about the ways you strive for balance in your personal and professional lives. What would it look like to instead establish a rhythm?

_____
_____
_____
_____
_____
_____
_____

The third leadership lesson #1 asserts that the "level of your sacrifice will determine the depth of the shift." What are you willing to sacrifice to make the shift happen?

_____
_____
_____
_____
_____
_____
_____

The fourth leadership lesson #1 says, "The Holy Spirit is your first and most loyal therapist/counselor." What does this look like practically in the face of difficult transitions?

_____
_____
_____
_____
_____
_____
_____

The fifth leadership lesson #1 is, "Until you have suffered or sacrificed beyond what Jesus sacrificed or suffered, you cannot claim victim status or quit." What is your knee-jerk reaction to this statement?

_____
_____
_____
_____
_____

The sixth leadership lesson #1 claims, "You're not the last man or woman standing. You never will be. There are others waiting to join you. Go find them!" Have you found others who are willing to stand with you? Who are they?

_____
_____
_____
_____
_____
_____

The seventh leadership lesson #1 states, "There must be a point at which you are willing to walk away." What are you holding onto that may conflict with the work God is trying to do?

_____
_____
_____
_____
_____
_____

What does the author's medical story tell you about God's call for us to rest even in times when rest doesn't make sense? In what areas of your life have you experienced this, and how might you find rest now?

The author lists several measures that need to be in place in order to properly care for yourself. Choose one item that you believe needs your attention. What adjustments will you commit to making?

The final leadership lesson #1 states that "there is never a time when you're not going to make it, no matter how dark and no matter how cold it gets." Have you found this to be true of your life? Explain.

CHAPTER 7

THE DIVINE NEW: MAVERICKS AND MANAGERS

> All leaders are managers, but not all managers are leaders.

READING TIME

As you read Chapter 7: "The Divine New: Mavericks and Managers" in *The Big Shift*, review, reflect on, and respond to the text by answering the following questions.

REVIEW, REFLECT, AND RESPOND

Consider Ecclesiastes 3:1-8. How do you know when a season is changing in your own life?

_____
_____
_____
_____
_____
_____
_____
_____

Do any of the seasons or "times" listed in this scripture align with where you are right now? What does that mean for you in relation to the decisions you are facing?

_____
_____
_____
_____
_____
_____
_____
_____
_____
_____

> *"Can two people walk together without agreeing on the direction?"*
>
> —Amos 3:3 (NLT)

Consider the scripture above and answer the following questions:

What is your process for arriving at an agreement with someone whose views and ideas you disagree with?

_____
_____
_____
_____
_____
_____
_____
_____
_____

Can you think of a time when a vision failed to materialize because of divergent beliefs between team players?

_____
_____
_____
_____
_____
_____
_____

What kind of influences (external influences, human innovation and progress, demographic changes, social movements, and advocacy) have informed the four types of change you've observed in your organization (evolutionary change, revolutionary change, technological change, cultural change)? How so?

_____
_____
_____
_____
_____
_____
_____
_____
_____
_____
_____

Think about your leadership style. Where do you see a manager, and where do you see a maverick?

_____
_____
_____
_____
_____
_____
_____
_____
_____

Of which of the four underlying reasons (fear of the unknown, loss of control, comfort with the familiar, past experiences) do you find yourself resisting change?

_____
_____
_____
_____
_____
_____
_____
_____
_____
_____

Who in your life challenges your limiting beliefs? To what degree do you actively challenge your own?

_____
_____
_____
_____
_____
_____
_____
_____
_____
_____

Consider the seven key strategies for setting achievable goals amidst uncertainty, with a special focus on breaking goals into smaller steps. What goals do you have that feel too big to accomplish, and how could you break them into smaller steps?

_____
_____
_____
_____
_____
_____
_____
_____
_____
_____
_____

How do your relationships fare in the midst of upheaval? Which ones are most challenging to manage, and what practices found throughout the book can you implement to strengthen those relationships when stress is high?

_____
_____
_____
_____
_____
_____
_____
_____
_____
_____
_____

CHAPTER 8

FISH, GOLD COINS, AND DOCTORS

> Stop chasing the crowd, or the one who everyone says you need, and chase the vision that God has put in your heart.

READING TIME

As you read Chapter 8: "Fish, Gold Coins, and Doctors" in *The Big Shift*, review, reflect on, and respond to the text by answering the following questions.

REVIEW, REFLECT, AND RESPOND

The first leadership lesson #1 in this chapter is, "Power and progress are found in unity, not methodology." Why is sound methodology insufficient for accomplishing a new vision?

_____
_____
_____
_____

What must believers do first before they can align in vision and mission?

_____
_____
_____
_____
_____

What has been your experience with chasing people who leave your organization because they are unhappy with the changes you made? What did you learn?

_____
_____
_____
_____
_____

> *"They were all in one accord, and the Spirit fell."*
> —Acts 2:4 (author paraphrase)

Consider the scripture above and answer the following questions:

What does this scripture say about unity as a contingency for the Spirit to do His work? Why does poor centrality between key players in an organization create a barrier to the Holy Spirit?

_____
_____
_____
_____
_____
_____
_____
_____

What does the process of living and working in one accord look like? What steps must be taken to arrive there?

_____
_____
_____
_____
_____
_____
_____
_____

The second leadership lesson #1 in this chapter advises to "stay committed to the standard of vision." What challenges have you faced in staying committed to your vision, and how did you overcome them?

_____
_____
_____
_____
_____
_____
_____
_____
_____
_____

Consider the third leadership lesson #1: "Discern the difference between diversity and division." Does your organization have a team member with a unique voice but is creating division? What needs to happen to bring unity to the group?

_____
_____
_____
_____
_____
_____
_____
_____
_____
_____
_____
_____

How united in mind and passion is your team? What do you think drives that unity or lack thereof?

_____
_____
_____
_____
_____
_____
_____
_____

How do you see the Holy Spirit moving in your church to create a body of one accord? In what ways does your church reflect the character of Christ?

_____
_____
_____
_____
_____
_____
_____
_____

Describe a time in your church when prayer brought about a "gold coin" moment. What came to pass, and what does it tell you about God's sovereignty over big shifts in your church and His faithfulness to fulfill His vision?

_____
_____
_____
_____
_____
_____
_____
_____
_____
_____

www.ingramcontent.com/pod-product-compliance
Lightning Source LLC
Chambersburg PA
CBHW062123080426
42734CB00012B/2965